D1799229

2

Jesus Christ is Good News.

By

John C Burt.

Photographs Courtesy of :

george - rosema.

tom - levold.

alex - block.

good - good - good.

liam - seskis.

Free Downloads on:

unsplash.com

CELEBRATE

GOOI

16

FOREWORD :

The title of
this book is :
' Jesus Christ
Is Good News?'
As a follower of

Him I do believe that He is the Good News that the World - at - Large is waiting for ! I ...

do not know
whether or not
you share this
view or if in fact
you have a
contrary view ?
However, it is

very important
for us all to
know where we
stand on this
Good News
about Jesus
Christ and why?

You in reality may never have thought through the issues about the Lord Jesus Christ ?

To myself, and many others the story of the Lord Jesus Christ is one of Good News for us and all of ...

humanity.

You may, have many, many questions, I found that the Lord Jesus Christ is able to answer them !

24

The great thing, is that, you can have your own encounter with the Lord Jesus Christ, He will meet you where you are at !

I want in this book to present the Lord Jesus Christ as the Good News that all have ...

watching and
waiting for ...
        The Son of
God became
flesh and
everything
changed in an
instant ! If your

up to it, read on
as we together
begin this
journey of
discovery and
education as to
all the Good ..

28

News about
the Lord Jesus
Christ ...

He only is
worthy of all
our praise and
adoration !

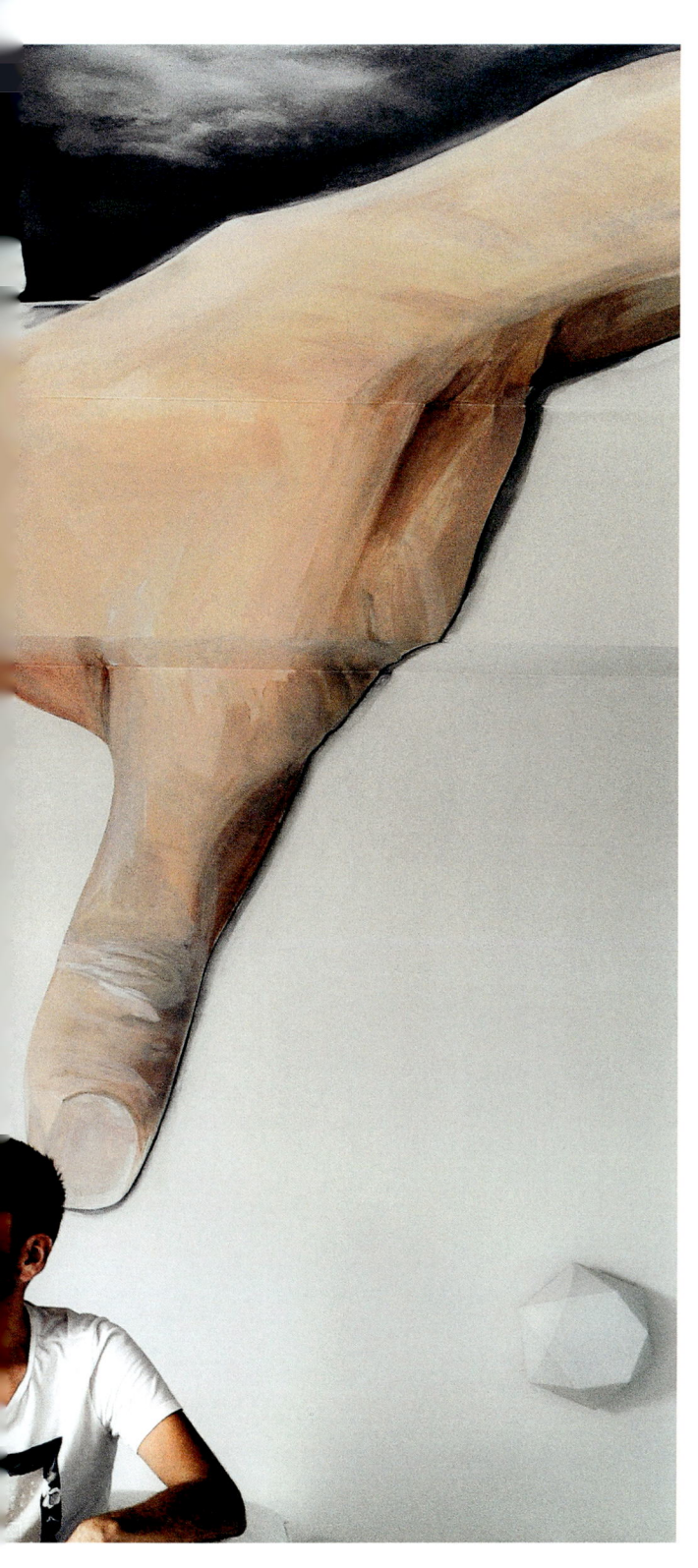

33

37

1.

We will now consider the various Scriptural Citations having to do with Jesus

Christ as Good News. To some degree, there is a play on words happening between the word for Gospel and that of Good News.

There will be four
different versions
of the various texts
given; they will be ,
the ESV, the NIV,
the MSG and the
GNT versions. This
is done in the
hope of greater

40

clarity as we consider the various texts from Scripture in this very book.

{ ESV }

Mark 1 : 15.

" (15) and saying,
" The time is fulfilled,
and the kingdom of
God is at hand; repent
and believe in the
gospel.""

Mark 10 : 18.

" (18) " And Jesus
said to him, " Why do
you call me good? No

one is good except God alone.""

Mark 16 : 15 - 16.

" (15) And he said to them, " Go into all the world and proclaim the gospel to the whole creation. (16) Whoever believes and is baptized will be saved, but whoever does not believe will be condemned." "

Luke 1 : 67 - 79.

Zechariah's Prophecy :

" (67) And his father Zechariah was

filled with the Holy Spirit and prophesied, saying,

(68) " Blessed be the Lord God of Israel,

for he has visited us and redeemed his people

(69) and has raised up a horn of salvation for us

in the house of his
servant David,

(70) as he
spoke by the mouth of
his holy prophets from
old,

(71) that we
should be saved from
our enemies
and from the
hand of all who hate us;

46

(72) to show mercy promised to our fathers

and to remember his holy covenant,

(73) the oath that he swore to our father Abraham, to grant us

(74) that we , being delivered from the hand of our enemies

might serve him
without fear,
      (75) in holiness
and righteousness
before him all our days.
      (76) And you,
child, will be called the
prophet of the Most
High;
      for you will go
before the Lord to
prepare his ways,

(77) to give knowledge of salvation to his people
in the forgiveness of their sins,
(78) because of the tender mercy of our God,
whereby the sunrise shall visit us from on high
(79) to give light

to those
who sit in darkness
and in the shadow of
death,
to guide our feet into
the way of peace.
(80) And the
child grew and became
strong in spirit, and he
was in the wilderness
until the day of his public
appearance to Israel.""

50

Luke 2 : 10 - 11.

" (10) And the angel said to them, " Fear not, for behold, I bring you good news of great joy that will be for all the people.
(11) For unto you is born this day in the city of David a Savior, who is Christ the Lord.""

51

Luke 6 : 45.

" (45) "The good person out of the good treasure of his heart produces good, and the evil person out of his evil treasure produces evil, for out of the abundance of his heart his mouth speaks.""

52

John 1 : 29 - 34.

Behold , the Lamb of God :

" (29) The next day he saw Jesus coming toward him, and said, " Behold, the Lamb of God, who takes away the sin of the world! (30) This is

53

he of whom I said,
' After me comes a man
who ranks before me,
because he was before
me. '
(31) I myself
did not know him, but for
this purpose I came
baptizing with water, that
he might be revealed to
Israel."

(32) And John bore witness: " I saw the Spirit descend from heaven like a dove, and it remained on him.

(33) I myself did not know him, but he who sent me to baptize with water said to me, ' He on whom you see the Spirit descend and remain, this is he who

baptizes with the Holy Spirit.'

(34) And I have seen and have borne witness that this is the Son of God." "

John 10 : 11.

" (11) " I am the good shepherd. The good shepherd lays ....

down his life for the sheep""

Romans 1 : 16.

" (16) " For 1 am not ashamed of the gospel, for it is the power of God for salvation to everyone who believes, to the Jew first and also to the Greek."

Romans 10 : 15.

" (15) And how are they to preach unless they are sent? As it is written, " How beautiful are the feet of those who preach the good news!""

1 Corinthians 15 : 1 - 2.

" (1) "Now I would remind you, brothers, of the gospel I preached to you, which you received, in which you stand,

(2) and by which you are being saved, if you hold fast to the word I preached to you - unless you believed in vain.""

1 Timothy 4 : 4 - 5.

" (4) For everything created by God is good,and nothing is to be rejected if it is received with thanksgiving, (5) for it is made holy by the word of God and prayer."

Titus 2 : 13 - 14.

" (13) waiting for our blessed hope, the appearing of the glory of our great God and Savior Jesus Christ, (14) who gave himself for us to redeem us from all lawlessness and to ...

61

purify for himself a
people for his own
possession who are
zealous for good
works."

**Revelation 14 : 6
- 7.**

" (6) Then I saw another angel flying directly overhead, with an eternal gospel to proclaim to those who dwell on earth, to every nation and tribe and language and people. (7) And he said with a loud voice, " Fear God and give him glory, because the hour of his judgment has come, and worship him who made heaven and earth, the sea and the springs of water." "

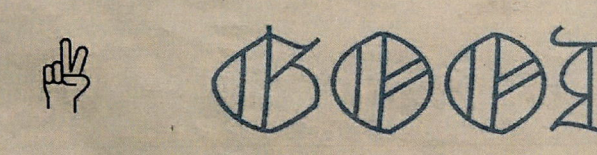

GOOD

CELEBRATE

2.

{ NIV }

Mark 1 : 15.

" (15) " The time has come," he said. " The kingdom of God has come near. Repent and believe the good news! " "

Mark 10 : 18.

" (18) " Why do you call me good?" Jesus answered. " No one is good - except God alone.""

71

Mark 16 : 15 - 16.

" (15) He said to them, " Go into all the world and preach the gospel to all creation.

(16) Whoever believes and is baptized will be saved, but whoever does not believe will be condemned. " "

72

Luke 1 : 67 - 80.

Zechariah's Song :

" (67) His father Zechariah was filled with the Holy Spirit and prophesied :
(68) " Praise be to the Lord,
the God of Israel,

because he has
come to his people and
redeemed them.
(69) He has
raised up a horn of
salvation for us
in the house
of his servant David
(70) { as he
said through his holy
prophets of long ago},

(71) salvation
from our enemies
and from the
hand of all who hate us
-
(72) to show
mercy to our ancestors
and to
remember his holy
covenant,
(73) the oath
he swore to our father

Abraham:

    (74) to rescue
us from the hand of
our enemies,
    and to enable
us to serve him without
fear
    (75) in
holiness and
righteousness before
him all our days.

(76) And you, my child, will be called a prophet of the Most High; for you will go on before the Lord to prepare the way for him, (77) to give his people the knowledge of salvation through the forgiveness of their sins, (78) because

of the tender mercy of
our God,
        by which the
rising sun will come to us
from heaven
                (79) to shine
on those living in
darkness
            and in the
shadow of death,
            to guide our feet
into the path of peace."

(80) And the child grew and became strong in spirit; and he lived in the wilderness until he appeared publicly to Israel." "

Luke 2 : 10 - 11.

" (10) But the angel said to them, " Do not be afraid. I bring you good news that will cause great joy for all the people.

(11) Today in the town of David a Savior has been born to you; he is the Messiah, the Lord. "

Luke 6 : 45.

" (45) A good man brings good things out of the good stored

up in his heart, and an evil man brings evil things out of the evil stored up in his heart. For the mouth speaks what the heart is full of."

John 1 : 29 - 34.

John Testifies About Jesus:

" (29) The next day John saw Jesus coming toward him and said, " Look, the Lamb of God, who takes away the sin of the world!
(30) This is the one 1 meant when 1 said, ' A man who comes after me has surpassed

me because he was
before me.'

(31) I myself
did not know him, but
the reason I came
baptizing with water
was that he might be
revealed to Israel."

(32) Then
John gave this
testimony: " I saw the
Spirit come down from

heaven as a dove and remain on him.

(33) And I myself did not know him, but the one who sent me to baptize with water told me, ' The man on whom you see the Spirit come down and remain is the one who will baptize with the Holy Spirit.'

84

(34) I have seen and I testify that this is God's Chosen One. " "

John 10 : 11.

" (11) " I am the good shepherd. The good shepherd lays down his life for the sheep. " "

Romans 1 : 16.

" (16) For I am not ashamed of the gospel, because it is the power of God that brings salvation to everyone who believes: first to the Jew, then to the Gentile."

Romans 10 : 15.

" (15) "And how can anyone preach unless they are sent? As it is written: " How beautiful are the feet of those who bring good news! " "

1 Corinthians 15 : 1 - 2.

" (1) Now, brothers and sisters, 1 want to remind you of the gospel 1 preached to you, which you received and on which you have taken your stand.

(2) By this gospel you are saved, if you hold firmly to the word 1 preached to you. Otherwise, you have ...

88

believed in vain. "

1 Timothy 4 : 4 - 5.

" (4) For everything God created is good, and nothing is to be rejected if it is received with thanksgiving,

(5) because it is consecrated by the

89

word of God and prayer."

Titus 2 : 13 - 14.

" (13) while we wait for the blessed hope - the appearing of the glory of our great God and Savior, Jesus Christ, (14) who gave himself for us to redeem us from all wickedness

90

and to purify for
himself a people that
are his very own, eager
to do what is good."

Revelation 14 : 6 - 7.

" (6) Then I
saw another angel
flying in midair, and he
had the eternal gospel

to proclaim to those who live on the earth - to every nation, tribe, language and people.

(7) He said in a loud voice, " Fear God and give him glory, because the hour of his judgment has come. Worship him who made the heavens, the earth, the sea and the springs of water ." "

GOO

@GOODGOODGOODCO   CELEBRATE G

3.

{ MSG }

Mark 1 : 14 -15.

" (14 – 15) After John was arrested, Jesus went to Galilee preaching the Message of God: " Time's up! God's kingdom is here. Change your life and believe the Message." "

Mark 10 : 18.

" (18) Jesus said,
" Why are you calling
me good? No one is
good, only God. " "

Mark 16 : 15 - 16.

" (15) ... Then
he said, " Go into the
world. Go everywhere
and announce the
Message of God's good

102

news to one and all.
Whoever believes and
baptized is saved;
whoever refuses to
believe is damned. "

Luke 1 : 67 - 80.

" (67 - 79) Then
Zachariah was filled
with the Holy Spirit and
prophesied,
Blessed be the Lord,

the God of Israel;
he came and set his
people free.
He set the power
of salvation in the
center of our lives,
and in the very
house of David his
servant,
Just as he
promised long ago
through the preaching

104

of his holy prophets:
      Deliverance from
our enemies
      and every hateful
hand;
      Mercy to our
fathers,
      as he remembers
to do what he said he'd
do.
      What he swore to
our father Abraham –

a clean rescue from the
enemy camp,
 So we can worship
him without a care in
the world,
 made holy before
him as long as we live.

And you, my child,
 " Prophet of the
Highest,"
will go ahead of the

Master to prepare
his ways,
Present the offer of
salvation to his
people,
the forgiveness of their
sins.
Through the heartfelt
mercies of our
God,
God's Sunrise will
break in upon us,

Shining on those in the
darkness,
those sitting in the
shadow of death,
Then showing us the
way, one foot at a
time,
down the path of
peace.
(80) The
child grew up, healthy

108

and spirited. He lived out in the desert until the day he made his prophetic debut in Israel."

Luke 2 : 10 - 11.

" (10 - 11).........
.....The angel said, " Don't be afraid. I'm here to announce a great and joyful event that is ....

meant for everybody, worldwide: A savior has just been born in David's town, A Savior who is Messiah and Master ....""

Luke 6 : 43 - 45.

" (43 - 45) " You don't get wormy apples off a healthy tree, nor good apples off a diseased tree. The health of the apple tells the health of the tree. You must begin with your own life - giving lives. It's who you are, not what you say and do, that counts. Your ..

111

true being brims over into true words and deeds."

John 1 : 29 – 34.

The God – Revealer :

" (29 – 31) The very next day John saw Jesus coming toward

112

him and yelled out,
" Here he is, God's
Passover Lamb! He
forgives the sins of the
world! This is the man
I've been talking about,
' the One who comes
after me but is really
ahead of me.' I knew
nothing about who he
was – only this: that my
task has been to get

Israel ready to recognize him as the God - Revealer. That is why I came here baptizing with water, giving you a good bath and scrubbing sins from your life so you can get a fresh start with God."

(32 - 34) John clinched his witness with this: " I watched the ......

Spirit, like a dove flying down out of the sky, making himself at home in him. 1 repeat, 1 know nothing about him except this :

The One who authorized me to baptize with water told me, ' The One on whom you see the Spirit come down and stay, this One will baptize with the Holy Spirit.' That's exactly what I saw happen, and I'm telling you, there's no question about it: This is the Son of God." "

John 10 : 11.

" (11) ... " I am the Good Shepherd. The Good Shepherd puts the sheep before himself, sacrifices himself if necessary ...."

Romans 1 : 16.

" (16) It's news I am most proud to proclaim, this extraordinary Message of God's powerful plan to rescue everyone who trusts in him, starting with Jews and then right on to everyone else! ....."

Romans 10 : 15.

" (15) ...." And how can they hear if nobody tells them? And how is anyone going to tell them, unless ....

someone is sent to do it? That's why Scripture exclaims,

A sight to take your breath away!
Grand processions of people
telling all the good things of God! " "

1 Corinthians 15 : 1 - 2.

" (1 - 2) Friends, let me go over the Message with you one final time - this Message that 1 proclaimed and that you made your own; this Message on which you took your stand and

120

by which your life has been saved. (I'm assuming, now, that your belief was the real thing and not a passing fancy, that you're in this for good and holding fast.) "

1 Timothy 4 : 4 - 5.

" (4 – 5) Everything God created is good, and to be received with thanks. Nothing is to be sneered at and thrown out. God's Word and our prayers make every item in creation holy."

Titus 2 : 13 – 14.

" (13 – 14) ...."This new life is starting right now, and is whetting our appetites for the glorious day when our great God and Savior, Jesus Christ, appears. He offered himself as a sacrifice to free us from a dark, rebellious life into this good, pure life, making us a people he

can be proud of,
energetic in goodness.""

Revelation 14 : 6 - 7.

Voices from Heaven :

" (6 - 7) 1 saw
another Angel soaring
in Middle - Heaven. He
had an Eternal Message

124

to preach to all who were still on earth, every nation and tribe, every tongue and people. He preached in a loud voice, " Fear God and give him glory! His hour of judgment has come! Worship the Maker of Heaven and earth, salt sea and fresh water! ""

GOOI

@GOODGOODGOODCO

CELEBRATE

4.

{ GNT }

Mark 1 : 15.

" (15) " The right time has come," he said, " and the Kingdom of God is near! Turn away from your sins and believe the Good News ! "

Mark 10 : 18.

" (18) " Why do you call me good?" Jesus asked him. " No one is good except God alone.""

Mark 16 : 15 - 16.

" (15) He said to them, " Go throughout the whole

world and preach the gospel to all people.

(16) Whoever believes and is baptized will be saved; whoever does not believe will be condemned." "

Luke 1 : 67 - 80.

Zechariah's Prophecy:

" (67) John's father Zechariah was filled with the Holy Spirit, and he spoke God's message:

(68) " Let us praise the Lord, the God of Israel!

He has come to the help of his people

138

and has set them
free.

(69) He has
provided for us a
mighty Savior,
a descendant of
his servant David.
(70) He
promised through his
holy prophets long ago
(71) that he
would save us from our

enemies,

     from the power
of all those who hate us.
     (72) He said
he would show mercy to
our ancestors
     and remember
his sacred covenant.
     (73 – 74) With
a solemn oath to our
ancestor Abraham
     he promised to

rescue us from our
enemies
        and allow us to
serve him without fear,
        (75) so that
we might be holy and
righteous
        before him all the
days of our life.
        (76) " You,
my child, will be called a
prophet of the Most .....

High God.
　　　You will go
ahead of the Lord
　　　to prepare his
road for him,
　　　　　(77) to tell
his people that they will
be saved by having
their sins forgiven.
　　　　　(78) Our
God is merciful and
tender.
142

He will cause the bright dawn of salvation to rise on us (79) and to shine from heaven on all those who live in the dark shadow of death, to guide our steps into the path of peace."

(80) The child grew and developed in body and spirit. He ..

lived in the desert until the day when he appeared publicly to the people of Israel.""

Luke 2 : 10 - 11.

" (10) but the angel said to them, " Don't be afraid! 1 am here with good news for you, which will bring great joy to all the people.

(11) This very day in David's town your Savior was born - Christ the Lord ! " "

Luke 6 : 45.

" (45) A good person brings good out of the treasure of good

145

things in his heart; a
bad person brings bad
out of his treasure of
bad things. For the
mouth speaks what the
heart is full of."

John 1 : 29 – 34.

The Lamb of God :

" (29) The next day John saw Jesus coming to him, and said, " There is the Lamb of God, who takes away the sin of the world! (30) This is the one 1 was talking about when 1 said, ' A man is coming after me, but he is greater than I am, because he existed before I was born.'

(31) I did not know who he would be, but I came baptizing with water in order to make him known to the people of Israel."

(32) And John gave this testimony: " I saw the Spirit come ...

down like a dove from heaven and stay on him.

(33) I still did not know that he was the one, but God, who sent me to baptize with water, had said to me, ' You will see the Spirit come down and stay on a man; he is the one who baptizes with the Holy Spirit.'

(34) 1 have seen it ," said John, " and 1 tell you that he is the Son of God." "

John 10 : 11.

" (11) " 1 am the good shepherd, who is willing to die for the sheep. " "

Romans 1 : 16.

" (16) I have complete confidence in the gospel; it is God's power to save all who believe, first the Jews and also the Gentiles. "

Romans 10 : 15.

" (15) And how can the message be proclaimed if the messengers are not sent out? As the Scripture says, " How wonderful is the coming of messengers who bring good news! " "

1 Corinthians 15 : 1 - 2.

" (1) And now 1 want to remind you, my friends, of the Good News which 1 preached to you, which you received, and on which your faith stands firm.

(2) That is the gospel, the message that 1 preached to you. You are saved by the gospel if you hold firmly to it –

unless it was for nothing that you believed. " "

1 Timothy 4 : 4 - 5.

" (4) Everything that God has created is good; nothing is to be rejected, but everything is to received with a ...

prayer of thanks,

(5) because the word of God and the prayer make it acceptable to God.""

Titus 2 : 13 - 14.

" (13) as we wait for the blessed Day we hope for, when the glory of our great God and

Savior Jesus Christ will appear.

(14) He gave himself for us, to rescue us from all wickedness and to make us a pure people who belong to him alone and are eager to do good.""

Revelation 14 : 6 -7.

The Three Angels:

" (6) Then I saw another angel flying high in the air, with an eternal message of Good News to announce to the peoples of the earth, to every race, tribe, language, and nation.

(7) He said in a loud voice, " Honor God

and praise his greatness! For the time has come for him to judge all people. Worship him who made heaven, earth, sea, and the springs of water !""

The easy way
reverse cha

Minimum charge (b)£3.48. Not available to some numbers
services. For pricing, terms and conditions call the BT
customer service number 0800 258 5000 or see www

No cash? No problem

Minimum fee 60p.

A Local or National cash
call for only 60p.

Please be prepared to use
no more than **four coins***
to pay the initial minimum
fee of 60p.

*BT payphones accept no more than 4 coins as the initial minimum fee pa
Additional coins can be added as the call progresses.

How much does a call cost? How can I pa, for a
To find out please phone 0800 345144

Payment

Customer Services

This phone is at:

(020) 7275-8869
O/S NUMBER 1214 BROAD
LONDON
E8 4QJ

Returned
Coins

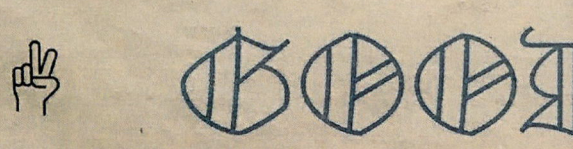

GOOD

CELEBRATE G

IEWSPAPER

BECOME GOOD NEWS.

ISSUE 01

5.

Now as this book proceeds we will give some time to

considering
some of the texts
that have cited by
it?

We will begin
with a look at
Mark 1 : 15 and
the words of the
Lord Jesus Christ?

Mark 1 : 15 { GNT}
" (15) " The right
time has come," he
said, " and the
Kingdom of God is
near! Turn away
from your sins and
believe the Good
News !"

172

It seems appropriate to begin with this text and the words of the Lord Jesus Christ ; from the very beginnings of His ministry? Firstly, note that He says it is the ' right time' for Him and His ministry upon the earth, to the people of Israel. The right time is significant and means a lot; there was a definite moment in time for the very coming of the Lord Jesus Christ. My point, is that, it did not just happen that he turned up on the scene of the history of the people of the Lord God Almighty. There was much thought and purpose in the very heart of the Father, in His coming and the start of His ministry to the people of the Lord God Almighty, Israel.

Furthermore, it is worth noting that He equates His

coming with the in -
breaking of the
Kingdom of God?
They had all been
waiting for the
coming of the
Kingdom of God and
here it was, with the
coming and the
ministry of the Lord

Jesus Christ. The thing to see, is that , the in - breaking of the Kingdom of God was very different from the Kingdom they were all expecting to happen and come to fulfillment ? What

178

the Lord Jesus Christ did later on, throughout His whole ministry is very different from what they expected the Kingdom of God coming to look and feel like. Yet, they had the prophets to

inform them all ,
what the Kingdom of
God the Lord Jesus
Christ was bringing
in would look like.
The reality, is simply
that they did not trust
or may be even
believe the prophets
of their ancestors?
180

In the last part of this verse , we have the idea of the Good News floated and announced by the Lord Jesus Christ. Here the Good News would seem to refer to the very coming of the

Lord Jesus Christ and even dare I say His ultimate death for the sins and wrongdoing of all humanity upon the Cross of Calvary.

The words ' turn away from your sins ' would seem to

182

be a call for real repentance on the part of the people ... Before the in-breaking of the Kingdom of God happens and the Good News of the Lord Jesus Christ upon the Cross takes place. It is reminiscent of the call to repent from sin and wrongdoing that the Lord Jesus Christ made throughout His very ministry upon the earth to all people He had contact with.

Finally, the
use of the words
' believe the Good
News ?' In many
ways, all the
Gospels are a
record of the very
battles for the belief
and believing of the
people by the Lord

Jesus Christ. Belief and believing the Good News are a core part of the in - breaking of the Kingdom of God and also they are caught up in repentance from sin and wrongdoing?

186

All of which, fits in with the themes of this particular book, and that is the need to believe that ' Jesus Christ Is Good News?' He was when He came and still is today in our times and our generations !

192

194

6.

We will now give a look at Luke 1: 67 - 80 and the Prophecy of Zechariah before

196

the birth of the Lord Jesus Christ. It has to do with his own son John the Baptist and yet, at the same time informs our discussion of Jesus Christ as Good News?

The Prophecy of Zechariah is worth noting and having a look at? It in many ways , reflects upon the very importance of both John and the

198

Lord Jesus Christ Himself and their coming into existence. The Prophecy sees the coming of the Lord Jesus Christ as the Lord God Almighty favoring the people of the Lord God. All of this would play out later in the very life, ministry and the ultimate death upon the Cross of Calvary of the Lord Jesus Christ. Zechariah pours out the Prophecy and it is a song of both praise and wonder for coming of both his son and the Lord Jesus Christ. In the end, through the coming of both his son John and the Lord Jesus Christ, Zechariah sees the Lord God Almighty sharing a part of His own glory with humanity - at - large and specifically with the very people of the Lord God Almighty themselves.

The Prophecy of Zechariah does not mince words ....

202

as to who the Lord Jesus Christ is and will be . ' (69) {GNT} " He has provided for us a mighty Savior, a descendant of his servant David." The Lord Jesus Christ was and is the Mighty Savior the Prophecy is referring to. The Lord Jesus Christ would be the one who would save the people of the Lord God Almighty from their sins and their wrongdoing before the Lord God Almighty. He also,..

has the 'right connections and lineage'; He is related to and from the house of David. They would have read this and seen very clearly that the Lord God Almighty had through this kept

the very real
promises He had
made to their father
David. The Lord God
Almighty had
promised His servant
David an eternal line
of descent and a
very continuation of
both his line and ...

reign as the King of Israel and the people of the Lord God Almighty. All of this was fulfilled through the birth and the coming of the Lord Jesus Christ to the people of the Lord God Almighty.

All of this, is filled out further for us all ...(73 - 75) {GNT} " he promised to rescue us from our enemies and allow us to serve him without fear , (75) so that ..

208

we might be holy and righteous before him all the days of our life." The enemies that it refers to; could be the last great enemy of death because of sin and wrongdoing? ...

The notion of being able to serve the Lord God Almighty without 'fear' would fit in with this concept and idea. It also foreshadows what the Lord Jesus Christ would do for the wrongdoing and sins of all humanity upon the Cross of Calvary.

All of this is heightened by verse 75 and what it has to say to us all? What is on show here is not the system of the sacrificial system of endless sacrifices;

sacrifices that have to be made and given to the Lord God Almighty in never ending processions. It seems to hint and foreshadow the one time sacrifice for wrongdoing and sin of the Lord Jesus Christ upon the Cross of Calvary.

Note as well, that this sacrifice that is being foreshadowed is one that affects the lives and times of everyday people. It's not just a ' right ' ...

standing with the Lord God Almighty at the end of their life that is on show. But rather, it is a righteous and a holiness that will and does impact the whole of their lives under the very gaze

214

of the Lord God Almighty.

All of which, is why I would believe the Prophecy and the Song that Zechariah has and gives is one that is both profound and telling in terms of the Good News ?

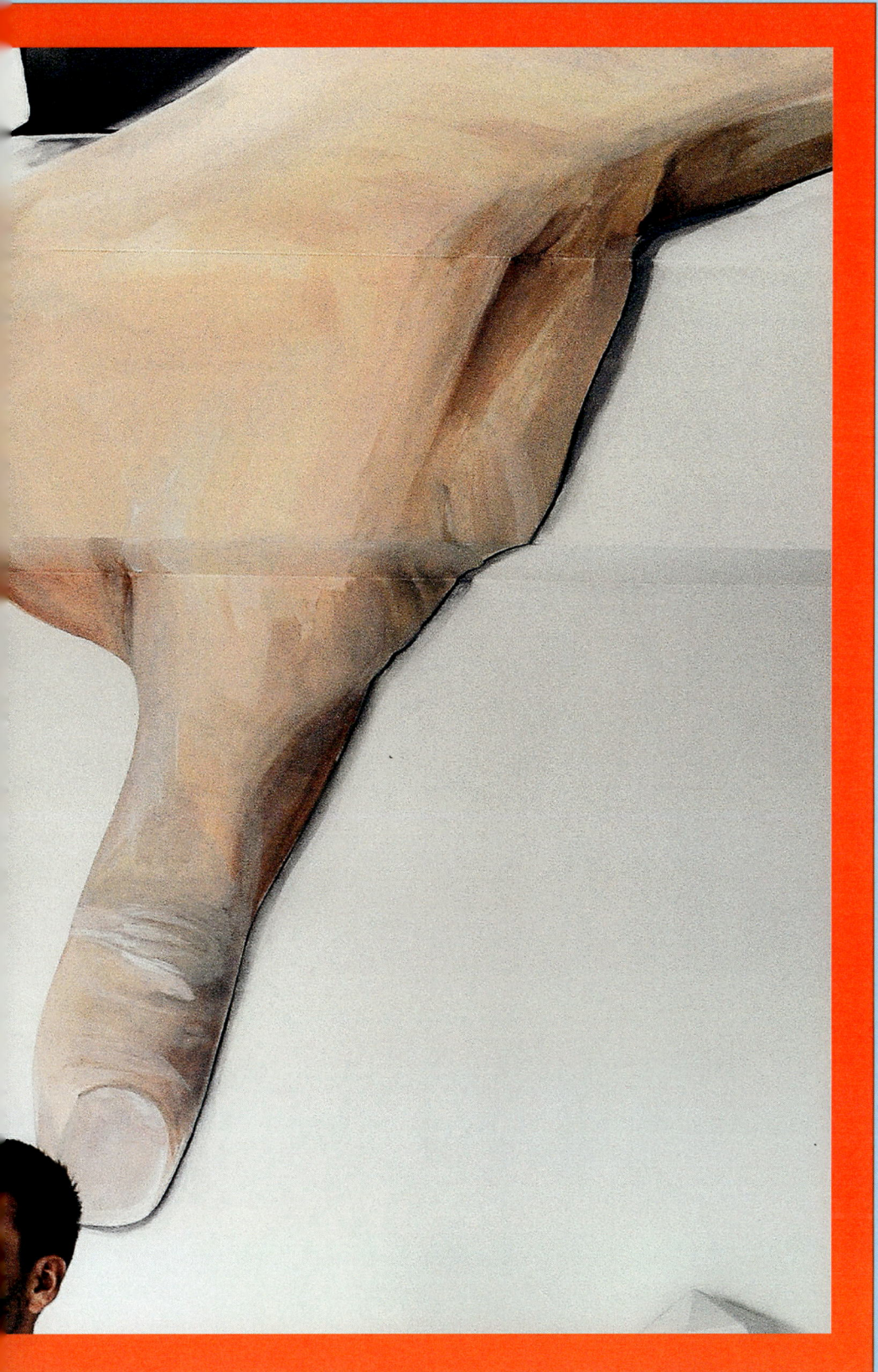

GOOD

CELEBRATE

NEWSPAPER

BECOME GOOD NEWS.

ISSUE 01

7.

At this point in this very book, 1 want to look at Luke 2 : 10 – 11 and what the ....

very Angel said
about the coming
birth of the Lord
Jesus Christ, in
the City of David,
Bethlehem? It's
all about it being
Good News.

Luke 2 : 10 - 11: {GNT} " (10) but the angel said to them, " Don't be afraid! I am here with good news for you, which will bring great joy to all the people.

226

(11) This very day in David's town your Savior was born - Christ the Lord! "

These words are given by the angel after the birth of the Lord Jesus Christ in Bethlehem. Again, we have the idea and notion of this birth of the Lord Jesus Christ in Bethlehem, David's town as being Good News not just for the people of the Lord God Almighty but for all people ?

228

Verse 11 fills out why this birth of the Lord Jesus Christ is Good News for all people. It is because He is the long awaited Savior; the One who had been promised to the people of the ...

Lord God Almighty. The One who has been born in David's town is designated by the very words of the angel as being the One who is both the Savior and the Christ the Lord.

The very words

of the angel at this juncture are directed towards shepherds in the fields who are just tending their sheep. The Lord God Almighty, the Father chooses to announce that the long awaited Savior has come to

the common and
everyday shepherds.
They were not
thought of as being
people of value and
worth and dignity
within the society
and community of
the times? All of
which reinforces the

notion that the very birth of the Lord Jesus Christ is in fact joyous and Good News for all people in the world - at - large. His birth is Good News for everybody, not just the people of God.

What we have been trying to do in the consideration of these verses from the various Gospels; is to see that the very birth of the Lord Jesus Christ was and is Good News for all peoples? It was and is Good News for those that were numbered amongst the very people of the Lord God Almighty but it goes far wider than just them and impacts all people's?

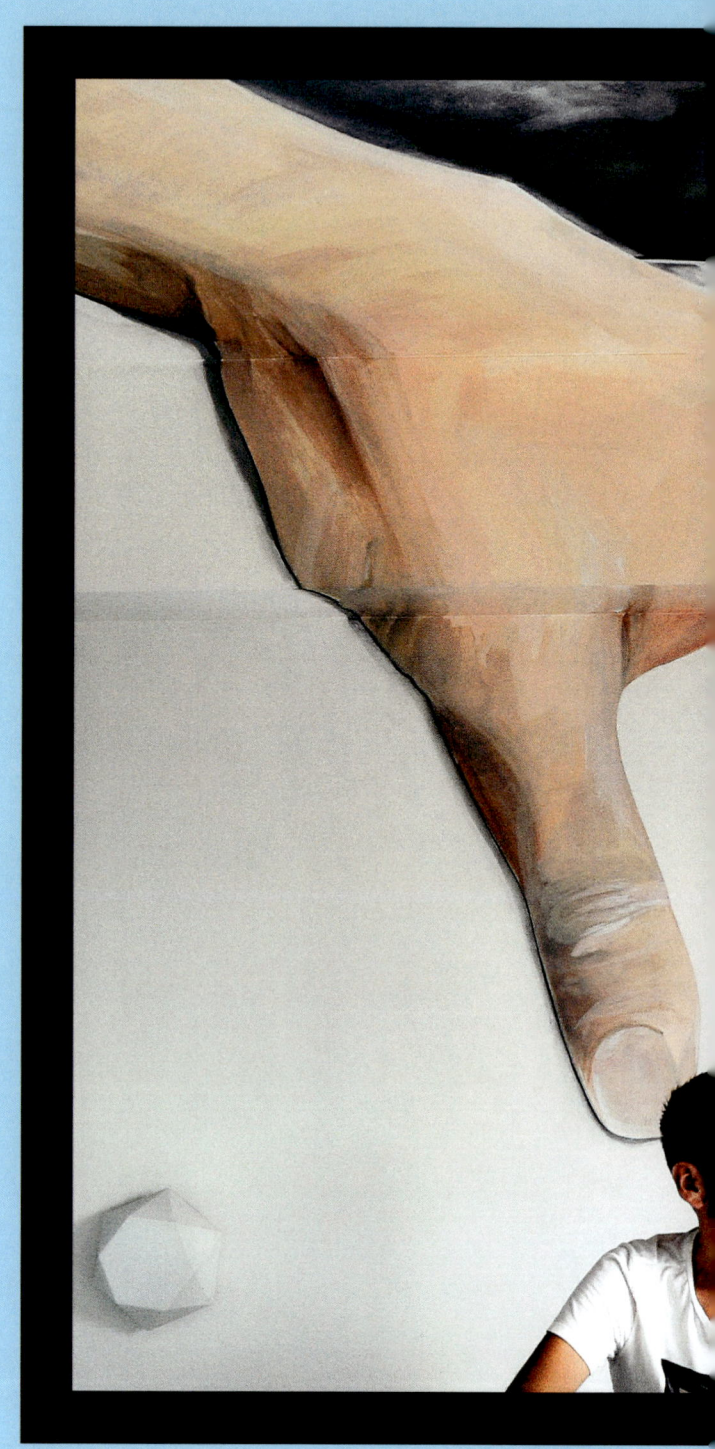

238

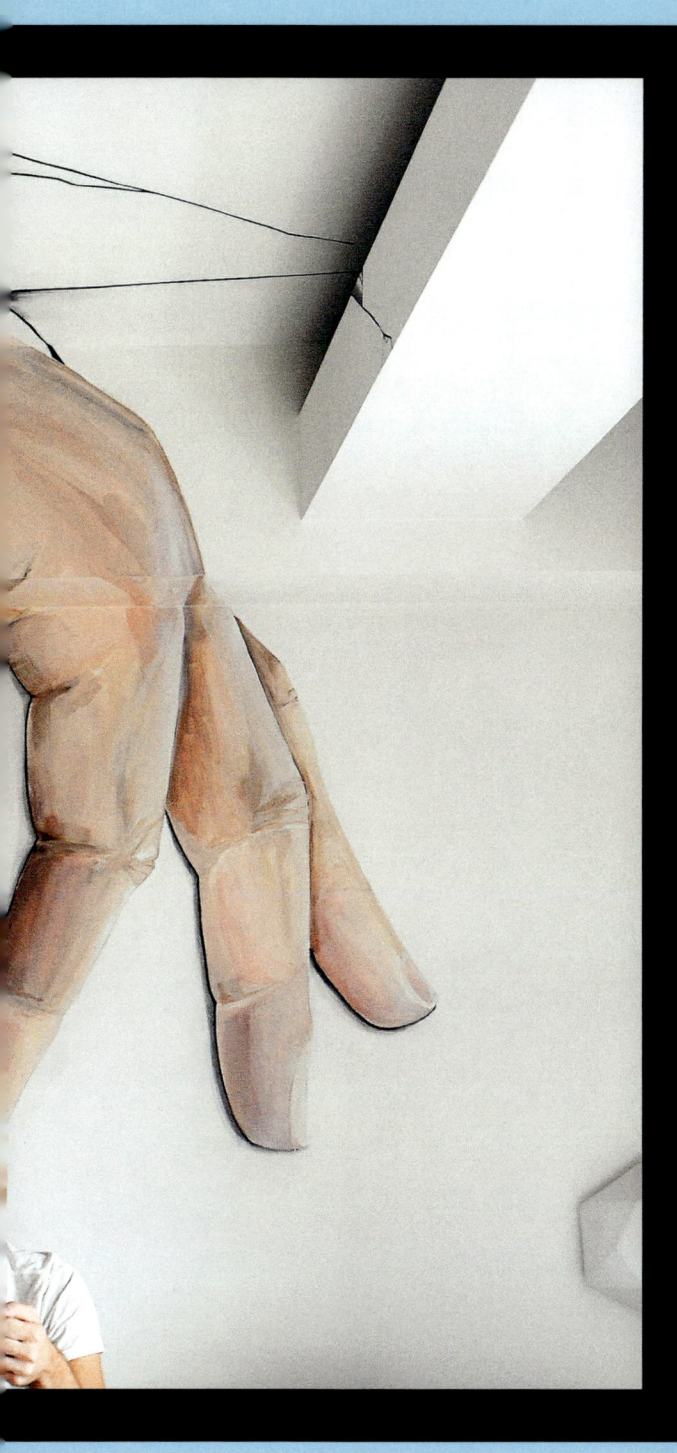

239

240

241

242

245

8.

We will now give some thought to John 1 : 29 – 34; as to what it has to say to us all in

terms of the Lord
Jesus Christ being
Good News for
the people of the
Lord God
Almighty and
everybody ? Good
News is on show!

John 1 : 29 - 34:
{ GNT } " (29) The
next day John saw
Jesus coming to
him, and said,
" There is the Lamb
of God, who takes
away the sin of the

world!

(30) This is the one I was talking about when I said, ' A man is coming after me, but he is greater than I am, because he existed before I was born. '

(31) I did not know who he would be, but I came baptizing with water in order to make him known to the people of Israel. "

(32) And John gave this testimony : " I saw

the Spirit come down
like a dove from
heaven and stay on
him.

(33) I still
did not know that he
was the one, but God,
who sent me to
baptize with water,
had said to me, ' You

will see the Spirit
come down and stay
on a man; he is the
one who baptizes
with the Holy Spirit.'
(34) I have
seen it," said John,
" and I tell you that
he is the Son of
God."

Forgive me for quoting these verses again but they are important to both see and understand regards the Good News that the Lord Jesus Christ was and is today? The forerunner John the

Baptist, saw the Lord Jesus Christ as being both the Lamb of God and the Savior of the World , as well as being the very Son of God.

It must be noted that John and Jesus Christ were in

fact cousins, and related to each other by their family lineage. Yet, even given this , the very words of John the Baptist about the Lord Jesus Christ and His appearance are both telling and profound to us all as the reader's of the Gospel of John, this is true even if we are removed from those times? John the Baptist knew from the Lord God Almighty that the Lord Jesus Christ ...

was in reality the one he had been preparing the people of the Lord God Almighty, Israel for.

The title that John the Baptist gives to the Lord Jesus Christ of the

Lamb of God hints and even foreshadows His sacrificial death upon the very Cross of Calvary for all humanity. It is His death upon the Cross that is and will be the perfect and without blemish or defect and the once for all sacrifice to the Father, the Lord God Almighty, as the payment for all the wrongdoing of all humanity.

The final title that John the

Baptist give the Lord Jesus Christ as the very Son of God , seals the deal. Not only was and is the Lord Jesus Christ the very Lamb of God but He is also the very Son of God.

260

The Lamb of God that has been supplied by the Lord God Almighty, the Father, is in reality His own Son, the Lord Jesus Christ.

   This divinity of the Lord Jesus Christ is seen clearly in the testimony of John the Baptist about the Holy Spirit coming upon the man the Lord Jesus Christ as a dove and remaining with Him and upon Him. All of this, the very involvement of the

262

Holy Spirit, sets the Lord Jesus Christ apart and marks Him as the very Son of God and the very Lamb of God, the One who has come from the Father, the Lord God Almighty ?

In conclusion, the Lord Jesus Christ, in the light of this very text from the Gospel of John, is both the Lamb of God and the very Son of God. All of which is why the Lord Jesus Christ is Good News for the people of the Lord God Almighty, Israel and everybody, all of humanity as well. It reveals very clearly that Jesus Christ Is Good News ?

266

267

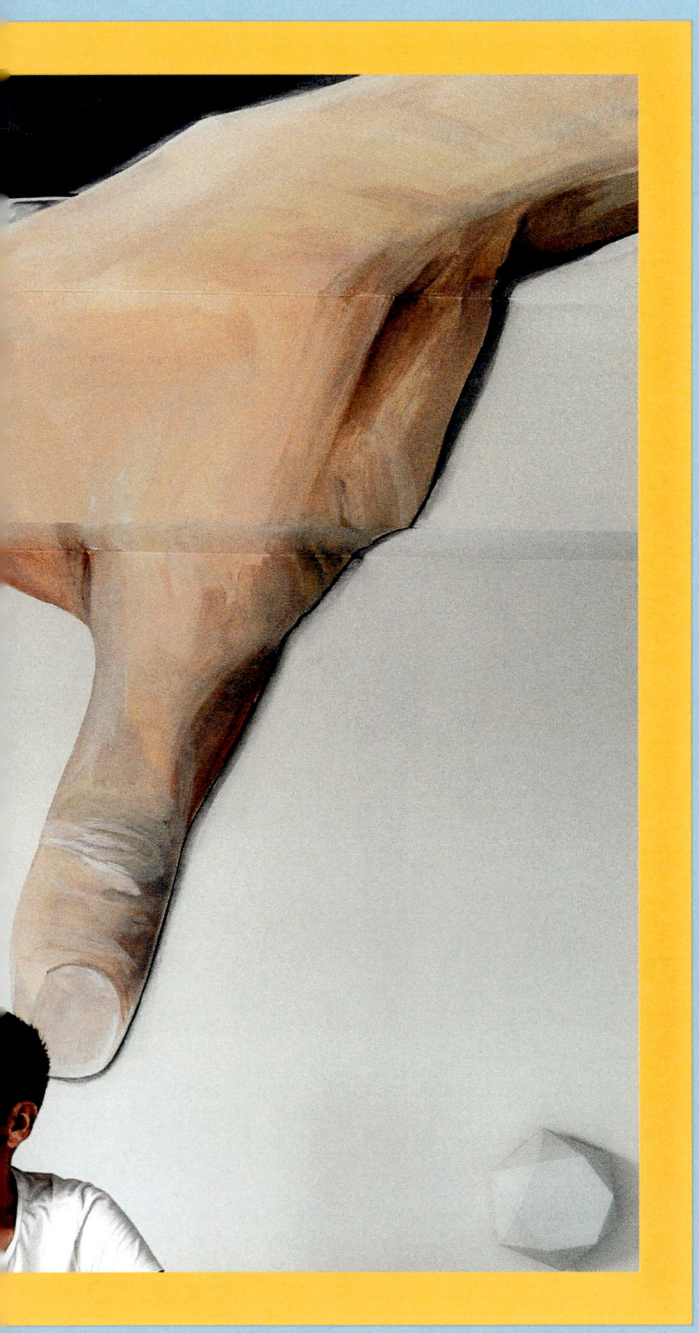

271

274

275

9.

At this moment;
we will examine
the verse from
Romans 1 : 16 ?

We will be thinking about how it relates to the themes of Jesus Christ being the Good News for both Israel and all people and humanity ?

Romans 1 : 16 :
{GNT} " (16) I have
complete confidence
in the gospel; it is
God's power to save
all who believe, first
the Jews and also

the Gentiles."

The question you are probably asking yourselves , is how does this very verse relate to the topic at hand in this very book? I pray to be able to provide an adequate answer to this very question within this chapter of the book.

Firstly, let us note that from the outset the Apostle Paul; who had a Pharisee of the Pharisee's has now complete confidence in the very gospel of the Lord Jesus Christ? This is in itself, a monumental shift of allegiance, thought and religious adherence by the Apostle Paul. One should not underestimate the shift and how massive it was for the Apostle Paul. He has been the Jew of the Jews before he encountered the risen Lord Jesus Christ of the road to

Damascus. This one encounter with the risen Lord Jesus Christ helped him become the Ambassador for the Lord Jesus Christ to the Gentiles of the known world - at - large. Paul left all of his former views of the Lord God Almighty and now saw the Lord Jesus Christ as being truly 'the Way, the Truth and the Life?'

Paul believes that the very gospel, of which he is now an

Ambassador , has the power to save all those who believe in it. First the Jewish people and then the Gentile people's will be saved by this very gospel he now preaches and adheres to. Because

of all of this, the
Apostle Paul would
have been one who
would have seen
the Lord Jesus
Christ as being
Good News for both
his people and all of
humanity - at -
large?

286

The point I want to focus on in this very chapter , is that, the Apostle Paul had put all his confidence, strength and belief in the gospel of the Lord Jesus Christ. He saw it as worthy of putting everything he had ...

into it. In the end, he is fully convinced and confident in the power of the gospel of the Lord Jesus Christ, of which he himself is an Ambassador , to save himself and others? In and with and through this very verse from the Letter to the Romans , the Apostle Paul does not seem or appear as a person who was wavering in their belief in the gospel and the Good News about Jesus Christ ?

Finally, if the power and the authority of the gospel of the Lord Jesus Christ was good enough for the Apostle Paul to have full confidence in, then, surely we can trust in it's saving power as well? In the end, it's another reason for us all to see ' Jesus Christ Is Good News?' He was for the Apostle Paul and countless numbers of believer's through the ages!

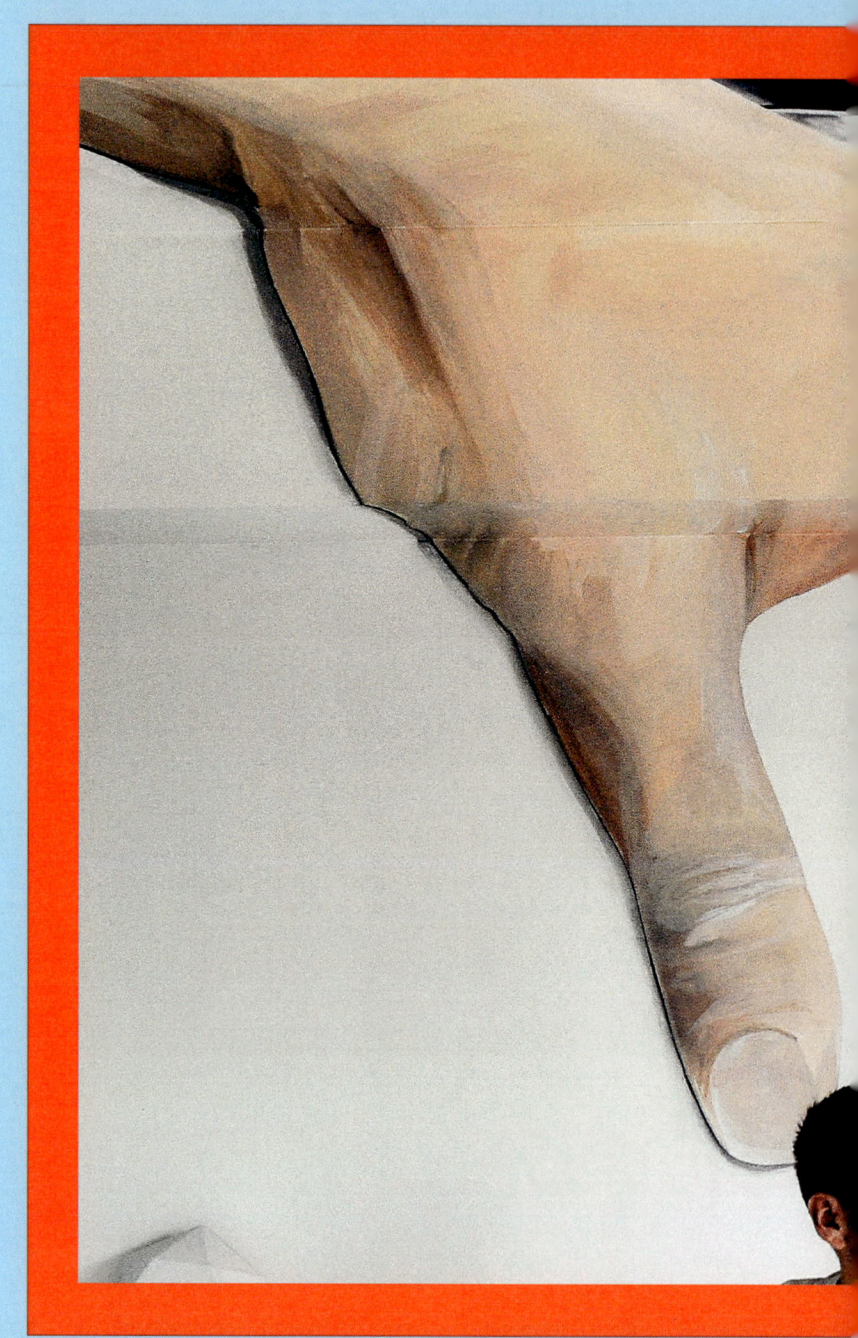

292

293

294

296

297

300

10.

As an introduction to the final verses to be looked at by this book , we will now look at Titus

302

2 : 13 – 14 and what it has to say to us about the Lord Jesus Christ being the Good News? He was and He will be the Good News for all people!

Titus 2 : 13 - 14 :

{ GNT } " (13) as
we wait for the
blessed Day we hope
for, when the glory of
our great God and
Savior Jesus Christ
will appear.

(14) He gave himself for us, to rescue us from all wickedness and to make us a pure people who belong to him alone and are eager to do good."

These verses from Titus 2 : 13 - 14 add to the Good News about the Lord Jesus Christ; there will be a Great and a Glorious Day of His return to earth. Not only, has

the Lord Jesus
Christ been Good
News because of His
dying for our sins
and our wrongdoing
before the Father but
also we eagerly
await His return to
earth. His return to
the earth, is caught

up with the full consummation of the Kingdom of the Lord God Almighty. The Kingdom of the Lord God will be fully realized when the Lord Jesus Christ returns in the second coming to the earth. This is Good News for all those who have put their faith, belief and very real hope in His returning to the earth, in His Second Coming. Not only has His death paid for all our wrongdoing and sins but also it involves and is caught with the very real hope of His return to the earth.

When He returns to the earth, thereafter the Church, the Universal Church, the Body of the Lord

310

Jesus Christ will be a people that will be His own people and treasured possession; to be all that they were meant from the Dawn of Time to be in and through Him? All of which, is much more than just our

311

wrongdoing's and our sins being forgiven. It hints at an eternal future and what it can and will look like for those who are found and abide in the Lord Jesus Christ. There is a hope and a very real future for those who are found to be in and through the Lord Jesus Christ. All of which, adds to the Good News that is, the Lord Jesus Christ !

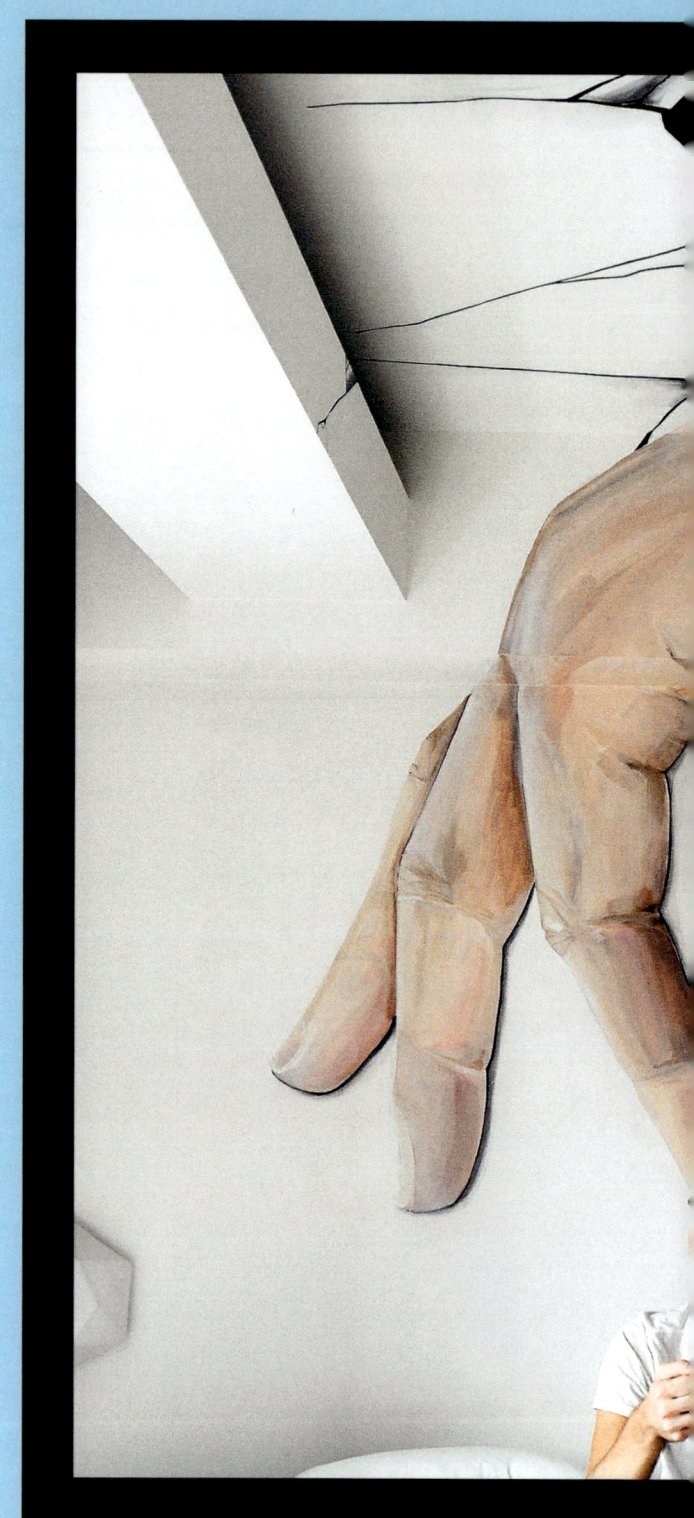

314

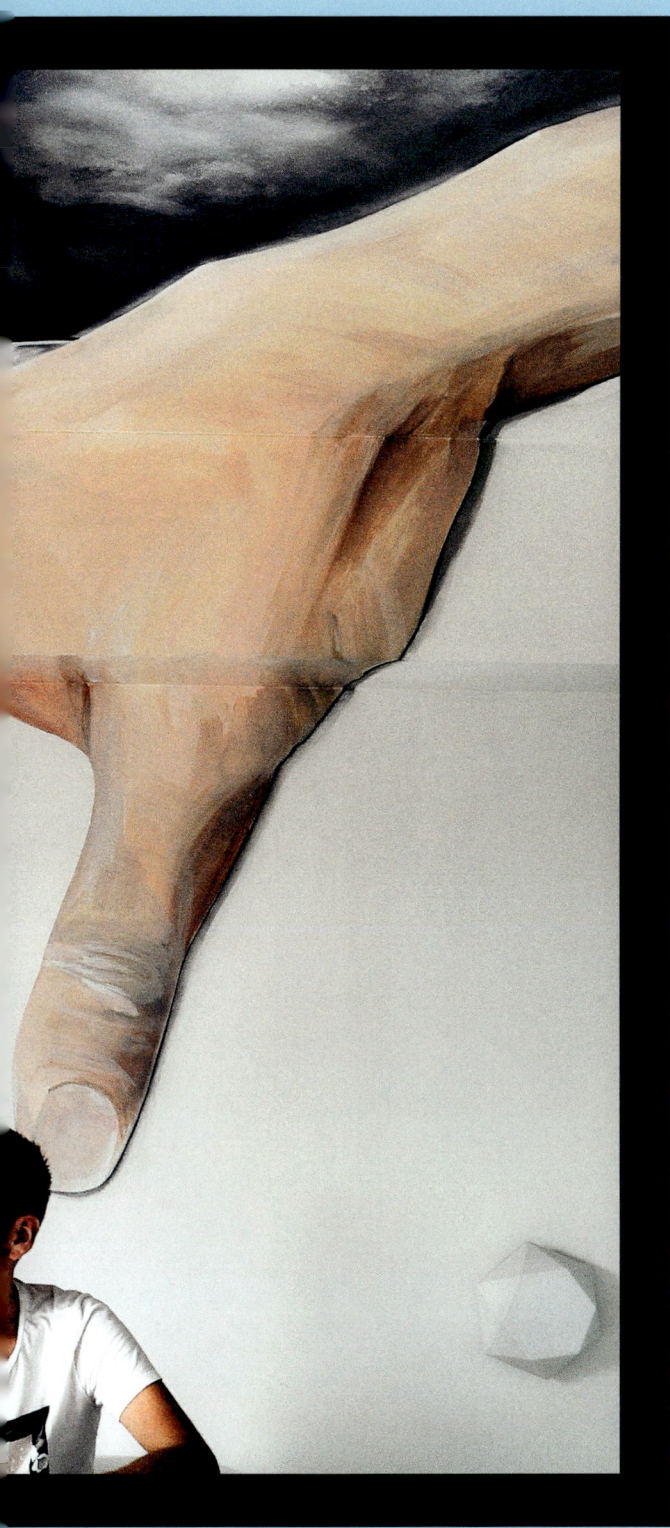

315

316

318

321

11.

In conclusion to our consideration of the texts cited , we will now look at Revelation 14 :

6 – 7, in terms of what it has to say to us all about the Lord Jesus Christ as the Good News ? The focus is on eternal things and the eternal Gospel !

Revelation 14 : 6 -7 :
{ GNT } " (6) Then
I saw another angel
flying high in the air,
with an eternal
message of Good
News to announce
to the peoples of the
earth, to every race,

324

tribe, language, and nation.

(7) He said in aloud voice, " Honor God and praise his greatness! For the time has come for him to judge all people. Worship ...

him who made
heaven, earth, sea,
and the springs of
water! " "

To some
degree, this might
seem to be a strange
way to finish a book
called :' Jesus Christ

Is Good News?' Yet, it is the time that the Good News of the Lord Jesus Christ is, was and will be about, in the end of all things. There will be a Day of Judgment before the Lord Jesus Christ that is a thing

we can all be
assured of
happening at the
end of time and
space, as we now
know it. If you have
accepted the free
gift of salvation and
forgiveness of your
wrongdoing and sins

through the very Cross of Calvary and the Lord Jesus Christ? Then you do not have to be too concerned about the Day of Judgment by the Lord Jesus Christ; your wrongdoing is covered and has been paid for !

The very real difficulty comes if you have not accepted and believed in the Lord Jesus Christ, His Cross and His Gospel and been forgiven of your own wrongdoing and sins? I do not know where you are at? But my prayer and very real hope , is that, both that ,you will be found by the Lord Jesus Christ and that this book has been a help in yourself coming to see and understand that the Lord Jesus Christ Is certainly Good News for you and all humanity - at - large.

The text ends with the very affirmation that it is

332

the Lord Jesus Christ, the Lamb of God and the very Son of the Living Lord God Almighty, the One who created all things, who alone is worthy of all praise, worship and adoration from humanity !

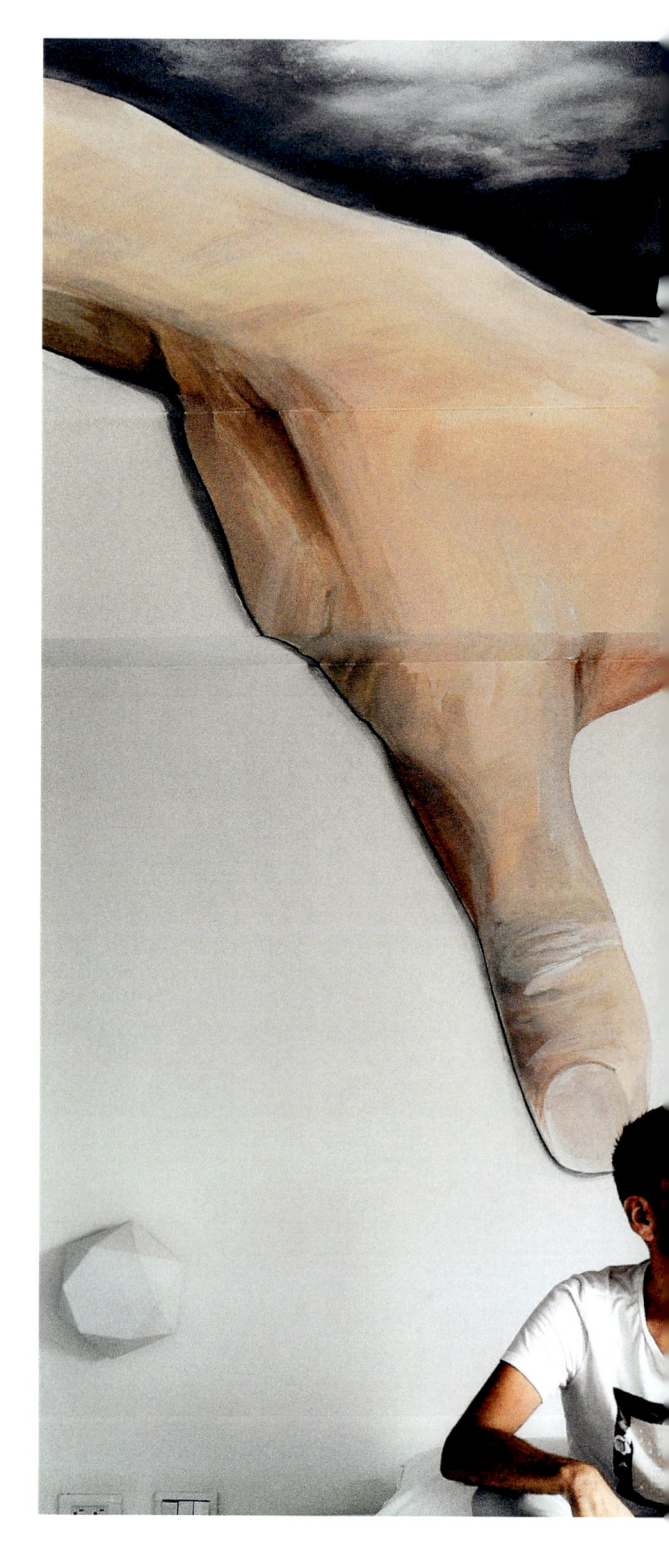

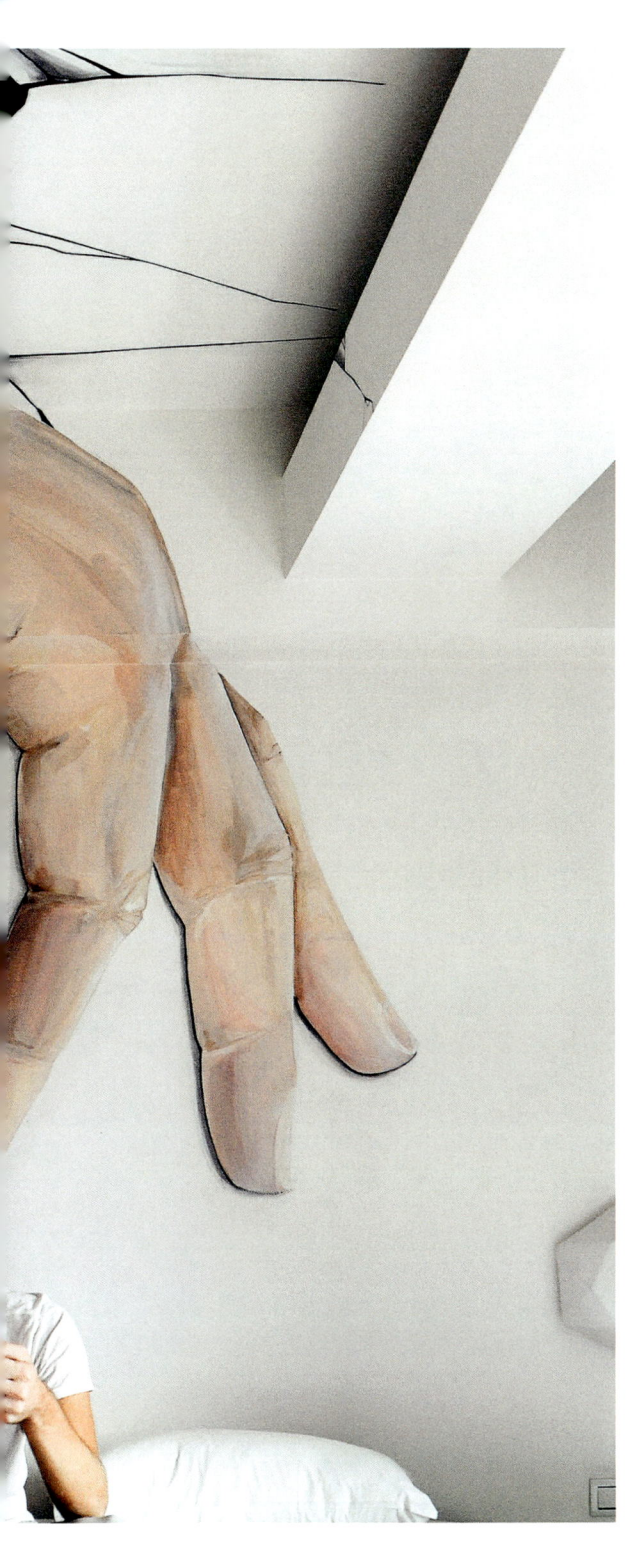

335

336

337

338

12.

EP1LOGUE :

We have
arrived at the end
of this book! My

real prayer, hope and even desire , is that, it simply has helped you in your walk with the Lord Jesus Christ; if you are already a follower of His? For others, my hope and prayer, is that, you can now simply see that ' Jesus Christ Is Good News?' It might well be something which you had some questions about?

I have tried to show that the Lord Jesus Christ is truly the One who is the Good News for all of humanity. He is the best News to ever come in terms of our relationship with the Lord God Almighty. Through Him and His Cross , we can be forgiven of all our wrongdoing and

sins. Set truly free to worship, adore and revel in the Lord Jesus Christ, the Father, and the Holy Spirit, for an eternity spent with them ....
AMEN !!!

The Author:
John C Burt

JOHN HAS BEEN
A FOLLOWER OF
THE LORD JESUS
CHRIST FOR
SOME FORTY -
THREE YEARS
AND STILL GOING
STRONG AND
GROWING !

348

JOHN LOVES FISH AND CHIPS, WITH FRESHLY CAUGHT FISH ... AS WELL AS PIZZA, AND THE ODD HAMBURGER AS WELL AS CUPS OF COFFEE !

349

A PRAYER YOU
COULD PRAY FOR
YOURSELVES IS :
DEAR LORD
JESUS CHRIST :
THANK YOU FOR
YOUR CROSS AND
FOR
FORGIVENESS OF

350

MY OWN
WRONGDOING
AND SINS. HELP
ME TO SHARE
THE VERY
REALITY OF YOU
BEING ' GOOD
NEWS ' FOR ALL
PEOPLE ! Amen!!!

AMEN

and

AMEN !!!

SHALOM!!!

353

354

356

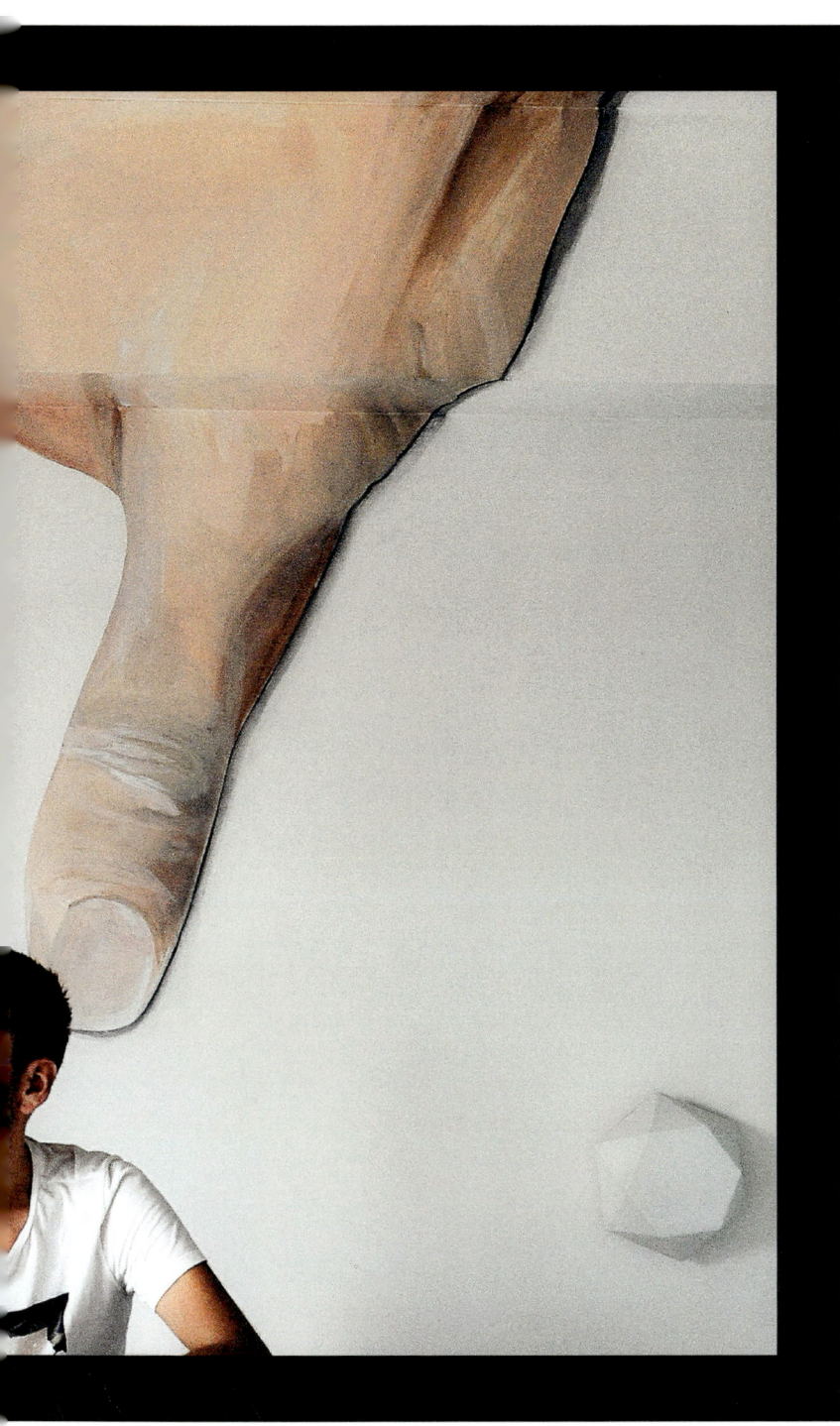

357

358